WOMEN and REVOLUTION
The living example of the Cuban Revolution

Asela de los Santos | Mary-Alice Waters

Arelys Santana | Leira Sánchez

I0112424

PATHFINDER

New York London Montreal Sydney

Copyright © 2013 by Pathfinder Press

ISBN 978-1-60488-048-9
Library of Congress Control Number 2012956139

Manufactured in the United States of America

First Edition, 2013
Fourth printing, 2026

COVER DESIGN: Eva Braiman

COVER PHOTOS: TOP: Havana, Plaza of the Revolution, December 1961. A hundred thousand literacy brigade volunteers, the majority of them young women, celebrate victory in year-long national campaign. Sign on top of building reads, "Cuba: Territory free of illiteracy." (*Granma*) BOTTOM: Havana, Plaza of the Revolution, January 2, 1961. Women's unit marches in first militia parade, on second anniversary of revolution's triumph. (Gilberto Ante/Roger Viollet/Getty Images)

PATHFINDER
pathfinderpress.com
Email: pathfinder@pathfinderpress.com

CONTENTS

Havana book fair 2012 'Women in Cuba: The Making of a Revolution Within the Revolution'

MARTÍN KOPPEL AND HARRY D'AGOSTINO

WOMEN IN CUBA: *The Making of a Revolution Within the Revolution*, published by Pathfinder Press, was launched at a packed auditorium here in Havana, February 14, 2012. The meeting, one of the hundreds of book presentations at the ten-day-long Havana International Book Fair, Cuba's biggest annual cultural event, drew one hundred thirty people from multiple generations. Among them were university students, including several youth from the United States studying in Cuba, members and leaders of the Federation of Cuban Women (FMC), and dozens of women and men who fought in the revolutionary war that overthrew the US-backed Batista dictatorship in 1959 and opened the socialist revolution in the Americas. The event was held at the Casa del ALBA cultural center in the heart of Havana.

The book, published in both English and Spanish, includes interviews with Vilma Espín, Asela de los Santos, and Yolanda Ferrer.

From the March 5, 2012, issue of the *Militant*, a socialist newsweekly published in New York.

Espín was a leader of the Cuban Revolution for more than fifty years, as a combatant of the July 26 Movement in Santiago de Cuba and the Rebel Army's Second Front in the mountains of eastern Cuba. After the 1959 victory she was the central leader of the revolutionary activity that gave birth to the Federation of Cuban Women. She was president of the federation until her death in 2007.

De los Santos, likewise a revolutionary combatant in the Santiago underground and Rebel Army, was a lifelong comrade-in-arms of Espín. A founding leader of the FMC, she served as its first general secretary and is currently a researcher in Cuba's Revolutionary Armed Forces Office of History.

Ferrer, who joined the FMC as a teenager in 1960, is its general secretary today and a member of Cuba's Council of State.[1]

Arelys Santana, second secretary of the FMC, who chaired the event, introduced the other three speakers on the panel: de los Santos; Leira Sánchez, a member of the National Bureau of Cuba's Union of Young Communists (UJC); and Mary-Alice Waters, president of Pathfinder Press and editor of the new book.

Santana also acknowledged the presence in the audience of several of the historic leaders of the revolution. These included revolutionary combatants such as Vice President José Ramón Fernández, Armando Hart, Brigadier General Teté Puebla, and Víctor Dreke.[2]

---

1. In October 2012 Ferrer was released from her responsibilities as general secretary of the FMC. Teresa Amarelle Boué, formerly first secretary of the Cuban Communist Party in the province of Las Tunas, replaced her.

2. For a photo and more information about many of these participants, see pp. 8–9.

Also participating were many founding leaders and long-time cadres of the FMC, including Carolina Aguilar, Alicia Imperatori, Iraida Aguirrechu, and Isabel Moya.

The speakers platform represents three generations of Cuban revolutionaries, Santana said. Waters's participation on the panel, she added, represents "the coming American Revolution, to recall the words of Jack Barnes," the national secretary of the Socialist Workers Party and author of the book *Cuba and the Coming American Revolution*. Waters and the SWP, Santana told the audience, are "comrades-in-arms, defenders of the Cuban Revolution who bring the facts about it to all platforms, especially over there in the heart of imperialism."

Leira Sánchez, the UJC's international relations secretary, stressed that the book tells a story "we have not always been able to write fully about," one that is an "important contribution to the new generations" in Cuba. Its "lively presentation makes it highly accessible to young people" who did not go through these experiences.

Sánchez said she first met Asela de los Santos several years ago when Sánchez was a student at the Enrique José Varona Teachers Institute of the University of Havana. De los Santos "spoke about everything that had been achieved in the Second Front in bringing to life the guiding program outlined in *History Will Absolve Me*. At that time it was virtually an unknown history for me," Sánchez recalled.

The UJC leader was referring to the Rebel Army's Second Front, commanded by Raúl Castro, which covered a vast rural territory in eastern Cuba freed from the control of the Batista regime. In the final months of the revolutionary war in 1958, de los Santos was placed in charge of the Second Front's Department of Education, which oversaw

Among the participants

Division General **José Ramón Fernández** commanded the main column of troops that defeated the US-organized Bay of Pigs invasion of Cuba in April 1961 in less than seventy-two hours of combat. Vice president of the Council of Ministers from 1978 to 2012.

Armando Hart, a founder and leader of the July 26 Movement, its national coordinator for a year before being captured in January 1958 by Batista's police. He served as Cuba's minister of culture for twenty years.

Brigadier General **Teté Puebla**, second in command of the Mariana Grajales Women's Platoon in the Rebel Army. Since 1985 she has served as director of the Office of Assistance to Combatants and Family Members of Internationalists and Martyrs of the Revolution.

Víctor Dreke, commander of the volunteer battalions that defeated the counterrevolutionary bands in the Escambray Mountains in the early 1960s, second in command to Ernesto Che Guevara in Cuba's internationalist mission to the Congo in 1965. Vice president of the Association of Combatants of the Cuban Revolution.

Carolina Aguilar, a founder and longtime leader of the Federation of Cuban Women. Director of Editorial de la Mujer, the publishing arm of the FMC, for many years.

Alicia Imperatori, founding administrator of the Ana Betancourt School for peasant women, organized by the FMC.

Iraida Aguirrechu, FMC founder and former longtime editor at Editora Política, the publishing house of the Central Committee of the Communist Party of Cuba.

Isabel Moya, FMC leader and current director of Editorial de la Mujer.

Longtime leaders of revolution occupied front row at presentation. **Top:** Front row, from right: Brigadier General Teté Puebla; Division General José Ramón Fernández; Armando Hart; Alicia Imperatori. Second row, from right: Isabel Moya (behind Fernández); Carolina Aguilar (applauding); Iraida Aguirrechu. **Bottom:** Part of audience at meeting, one of hundreds of book presentations at 2012 fair.

the opening of more than 400 primary schools and the initiation of literacy classes for rebel combatants and others.

History Will Absolve Me was Fidel Castro's courtroom defense speech at his 1953 trial for having led an attack on the dictatorship's army barracks in the cities of Santiago and Bayamo. It became the political program of the July 26 Movement, outlining basic social, economic, and democratic measures that the revolutionary government would implement.

Social revolution led by Rebel Army

De los Santos told the audience that the efforts waged in the Second Front were the forerunner of "the great revolution in education we launched after the victory" of January 1959, beginning with the mobilization of 100,000 young volunteer teachers, most in their teens, who spread out across rural Cuba to teach nearly a million women and men to read and write. They wiped out illiteracy in Cuba within a year.

De los Santos quoted from Waters's introduction to the book:[3] "In the firsthand accounts of Asela de los Santos and Vilma Espín, we see the interaction between the Rebel Army combatants and the exploited, landless peasants and agricultural workers of the region. We see the ways in which they transformed each other and together became a stronger, more conscious revolutionary force." That paragraph, de los Santos said, "gets to the heart" of the social revolution led by the Rebel Army.

She noted that the involvement of women in the Cuban Revolution began "with the significant numbers of women

3. See p. 46.

in the ranks of the Rebel Army" and "Fidel's leadership in the struggle for equality."

Following the revolutionary victory, "in the early days we spoke only of women's participation," she said. But "through that simple, concrete, yet by no means easy work, the first steps were being taken in the complex and long battle for the full equality for women."

De los Santos concluded by saying that the book itself underscores "our determination to remain united, working for the revolution—both here in Cuba and there in the United States."

Book needed by workers in struggle

Waters thanked the leadership of the Federation of Cuban Women and the Association of Combatants of the Cuban Revolution for their collaboration in making possible *The Making of a Revolution Within the Revolution*, a four-year effort.

She focused her remarks on why the new book "is important in the United States and elsewhere outside Cuba to the increasing numbers of workers who are searching for ways to effectively resist, and end, intensifying assaults by the capitalist owners of the means of production and their government on the wages, job conditions, and rights of working people."

"The living example of the men and women who made the Cuban Revolution, and are still making it, needs to be known," Waters said, "because working people everywhere, sooner or later, will be pushed toward revolutionary action."

More than one hundred copies in both Spanish and English of *The Making of a Revolution Within the Revolution* were sold at the presentation, and nearly fifty more during the course of the book fair. Presentations of the book after the fair were organized by the Association of Combatants of the Cuban Revolution and by the Union of Young Communists and Federation of University Students. The February 14 event was covered by *Granma* and *Juventud Rebelde*, Cuba's two daily newspapers, as well as other news services.

The full text of the remarks by Santana, de los Santos, Sánchez, and Waters follows.

'Our revolution: Neither an imitation nor a copy'

ARELYS SANTANA

GOOD AFTERNOON, EVERYONE. I'd like to introduce you to today's panel.

We have Asela de los Santos Tamayo, Rebel Army combatant, Heroine of Labor, and currently a researcher at the Revolutionary Armed Forces Office of History.

Leira Sánchez Valdivia, member of the National Bureau of the Union of Young Communists.

Mary-Alice Waters, president of Pathfinder Press and editor of *New International*.

And I cannot forego saying that among the many who have joined us for this very special day are our beloved Armando Hart and José Ramón Fernández.

Our panel today presents a book that is a genuine contribution to the history of the revolution—as you who decide to enjoy it will be able to confirm for yourselves. This is because—as its editor, Mary-Alice Waters explains—it is not about women, but rather focuses on the millions of Cuban women and men who carried out

---

Arelys Santana is second secretary of the Federation of Cuban Women.

and continue to make a revolution.

Women in Cuba: The Making of a Revolution Within the Revolution transmits a clear and accurate vision of our revolution in all its dimensions: economic, political, cultural and social.

This panel, which I would call exceptional, will speak about the merits of this work and why it should attract the attention of both men and women. I am honored that the National Secretariat of the Federation of Cuban Women has asked me to participate. Compañera Yolanda Ferrer Gómez, general secretary of our organization and one of the authors of the book, was originally to have been part of the panel. But unavoidable international responsibilities made that impossible, and she asked me to bring you her greetings.

We are joining our close friend Mary-Alice Waters, whose publishing house, Marxist by training and thinking, has just completed the rigorous and consciously revolutionary undertaking of producing this book. They have dedicated many years of labor traveling to our country, researching and reading, visiting the institutions that preserve material of great value and authenticity, to arrive at this point. It is being presented today in Cuba, and surely very soon it will be in New York, London, Montreal, Sydney, in other American cities, and even in other countries.

Mary-Alice, the publishing house she is president of, and the Socialist Workers Party of the United States, of which she is a leader, are comrades-in-arms, defenders of the Cuban Revolution who bring the facts about it to all platforms, especially over there in the heart of imperialism.

Each panelist will present her impressions of the book. Asela will talk about the merit of its contents. She will

MAURA DELUCA/MILITANT

At presentation of book in Havana, February 2012. From left: Leira Sánchez, member of National Bureau of Union of Young Communists; Asela de los Santos, one of book's authors; Arelys Santana, second secretary, Federation of Cuban Women; Mary-Alice Waters, book's editor, president of Pathfinder Press.

"This isn't a book about women," Santana said, citing its introduction. "It's about the millions of Cuban women and men who made, and continue to make, the revolution."

give a firsthand account as a front-line leader of what is the main theme of the book: the revolution of Cuban women within the socialist revolution.

This exceptional panel not only joins together US and Cuban women in the same cause, it also unites three generations of Cubans who personify the continuity of our revolution—from Asela, who was part of initiating the process, to those of us who, together with the founding nucleus, carried it forward. We are united in our determination to continue making that revolution. The authors and editors represent both a decisive part of the Cuban Revolution and, in the words of Jack Barnes, of the coming North American revolution as well.

I am certain that I express the feelings of Mary-Alice and Leira, of the participants, among them Fernández and Hart, when I say that this event is exceptional also because of the presence of Asela de los Santos Tamayo, one of the founders of our new nation and its institutions, of Cuba's socialist society, the great accomplishment of our revolution.

Asela really does not need any introduction here. We, the members of the Federation of Cuban Women, however, always wish to do so to express our respect, our affection, and our gratitude for her commitment and her talents, which have always been placed at the service of the people. She is a true *santiaguera* [woman of Santiago de Cuba], a patriot, and a revolutionary.

"To extend honor does one honor," our great teacher José Martí told us,[1] and while we do not wish to offend your

---

1. José Martí (1853–1895), Cuba's national hero. He led the fight against Spanish colonial domination and US designs on the island. He organized the 1895 independence war and was killed in combat.

modesty, Asela, we revolutionary Cuban women of these times feel truly represented by you.

One of the virtues of the book is the vivid and faithful picture of the authors that Mary-Alice provides, both in the biographical data and in the interviews themselves. Those who read it and become acquainted for the first time with the details of the lives of Vilma, Asela, and Yolanda will understand better their iron will, the daring and courageous spirit of the two combatants from the time of the revolutionary war, and their work in building socialism. They helped bring to life the prediction of the Peruvian communist José Carlos Mariátegui, who affirmed that revolutions in our Americas would be neither imitations nor copies, but instead processes of heroic creation.

Our very Cuban synthesis of the best patriotic traditions, of the continuity of the dreams of revolutionaries of all times, not only fulfills Mariátegui's prediction. It also reaffirms the conviction of Fidel and Raúl that, ¡Sí se puede! Yes we can! It is possible to build a better world that erases the wounds of the past. It is possible to build a society of justice and equality in which both women and men are more educated, more free.

'Years of intense life and accelerated learning'

ASELA DE LOS SANTOS

PARTICIPANTS IN THIS presentation, especially members of the Federation of Cuban Women—and that includes you, Mary-Alice:

Arelys announced that I would speak about the merits of this book. And so I will, but not only because I was invited to do so as a person interviewed in it. I also address you as a reader, a reader who very much wishes to express her opinions about the results of a publishing effort on a topic that was chosen by the author and her publishing house. That project—the Cuban Revolution and the role played in it by women—is the book we present today.

I believe the first indisputable merit of this book lies in its overall conception, its form and content. It contains four carefully selected interviews that focus on the central theme. Each interview is accompanied by information essential to understanding its time and context.

The result is a work that presents the political ideas of the Cuban Revolution and the unique way it put them into practice in society, bringing to reality the aspirations and dreams of so many generations of Cuban women and men.

For me personally it was a welcome exercise to retrace, in reading this book, the thorny path of the political and educational work that was part of instilling the ideas of equality and justice, of liberation and freedom, consistent with the revolutionary concepts we had drawn from Martí, Marx, and Fidel [Castro]. To retrace the great and multiple efforts we undertook to make the essence of these ideals part of the blood and bone of every individual among our people.

I also consider as a fundamental merit—alongside the wealth of information it offers—the book's inviting appearance, the quality of its graphic design, one more aspect that makes it so attractive. It's a book of unquestionable professional rigor: diligent, thorough, and carefully thought out to the smallest detail. The interviews are well chosen, the product of an arduous review of a vast amount of published material. The "Débora" interview with Vilma,[1] conducted by the editors of *Santiago*, the magazine of the University of Oriente, in 1975 to mark International Women's Year, has become a central document in the history of the Cuban revolutionary movement in the second half of the twentieth century.

In this first part of the book, the editors emphasize the stage of the insurrectional struggle, focusing on actions carried out by underground combatants in the former Oriente province and its capital, Santiago. Their effort to clarify events, participation, background, tasks, results, assessments, and personal responsibilities, right to the end of the revolutionary war, more than succeeded.

---

1. "Débora" was the nom de guerre used by Vilma Espín during much of the revolutionary war.

"In Asela de los Santos's sketch of the veritable 'republic in arms' established, under the leadership of the Rebel Army, by peasants and workers in the territory of the Second Front, we see the whole future course of the revolution," said Waters.

Left: De los Santos (left) with Zoila Ibarra, assistant head of Rebel Army's Education Department, Second Eastern Front, late 1958. **Below:** De los Santos signing copies of book after presentation, February 2012.

I also appreciate the careful preparation that was done for the interview that Mary-Alice Waters and Martín Koppel conducted with me in 2008 and completed in 2009 and 2010. It had to be done with great care because the two interviews, the one with Vilma and the one with me, address the same issues yet still complement each other. In my case, they offered me the opportunity to take up details on which little has been published. That included the organization of actions taken in the liberated territory of the Frank País Second Eastern Front, under the command of Raúl [Castro], and in which Vilma shouldered important responsibilities.

Commander Raúl Castro assigned me responsibility for education. I explain this in detail in the book, which I hope you have a chance to read, because the steps we took were not only interesting and necessary. They were also the basis for the great revolution in education we began after the victory.

To sum up, the first part of the book takes up the experiences of women and men engaged in revolutionary activity, particularly in Santiago de Cuba and throughout Oriente province. I can assure you that it provides a direct, firsthand account of those years of intense life, of accelerated learning from all the battles of the revolutionary war, of acquiring political consciousness, of gaining firsthand knowledge of the harsh realities of the country, of our personal development, of the deepening among us of the most universal values of human beings. There, in the mountains and in the underground groups, equality and fraternity, solidarity and friendship, truth and justice, work, generosity, and respect for human dignity prevailed over the mediocrity, pettiness, selfishness, and prejudices of all types that were imposed by the times of slavery, rooted in mind and behavior by centuries of colonial rule.

In the second part of the book, the interviews with Yolanda Ferrer and Vilma explain in detail every action, every task, every mission of the Federation of Cuban Women since its conception and entry into activity. They make clear that the basis for this was the experience we had been part of in Cuba—the numbers of women in the ranks of the Rebel Army, the mass movement that was built everywhere in support of the revolution.

Here, in this part of the book, you can appreciate a quality that Mary-Alice stresses: social practice that matches political theory—that is, our revolution's consistent course of fighting for equality. It's true that in the early days we spoke only of participation of women as the strategic objective. But the breakdown of barriers between the private and the public that came with women stepping out from their traditional areas and duties—homemaker, the one responsible for all family matters, the mother and wife— that simple, concrete, but in no way easy step laid the initial groundwork for the big, complex battle for the full exercise of women's equality.

In her introduction—which I consider an excellent, rigorously Marxist work, one that could well be included among the basic documents to be developed further—Mary-Alice points to all these challenges as essential parts of the social revolution.[2]

I would like to quote a paragraph that reflects her keen eye, that gets to the heart of things: "In the firsthand accounts of Asela de los Santos and Vilma Espín, we see the interac-

---

2. The introduction is reprinted as the last item in this book.

"In the underground groups and in the mountains, those were years of gaining firsthand knowledge of the harsh realities of our country," said Asela de los Santos.

Above: Rebel Army combatants at entrance to general command center, early 1958, Guayabal de Nagua, Sierra Maestra mountains. From left, Clodomira Acosta, Rebel Army messenger later arrested, tortured, and murdered by Batista's police; Pilar Fernández, teacher who collaborated with underground movement in Manzanillo, later assigned to work with Celia Sánchez (in doorway), member of Rebel Army general staff; others are unidentified.

Havana

C U B A

Santiago de Cuba

Guáimaro

Victoria de
las Tunas

HOLGUÍN

C A M A G Ü E Y

O R I E N T E

Río Cauto

4

Manzanillo

Bayamo

Buey Arriba

1

3

Mi

Palm
Sorianc

S I E R R A   M A E S T R

La Plata
command
center

Cuban Revolutionary War Eastern Fronts, Late 1958

First front established December 1956, Cmdr. Fidel Castro.
Second front established March 1958, Cmdr. Raúl Castro.
Third front established March 1958, Cmdr. Juan Almeida.
Fourth front established October 1958, Cmdr. Delio Gómez Ochoa.

1, 2, 3, 4 FRONTS
■ ■ ■ Front boundaries
CENTRAL HIGHWAY
Smaller roads
— — — — Country roads
Railroad tracks
▪▪▪▪▪▪▪ Provincial boundary
● Larger city
◉ All other cities, towns and villages
🏴 Rebel Army command center
✕ Nickel mine
⚒ Sugar mill
★ Headquarters of Second Front

Banes

Atlantic Ocean

Moa

Mayarí
Nicaro
SIERRA CRISTAL

Tumba Siete
★ Mayarí Arriba
SAGUA BARACOA MOUNTAINS

Baracoa

San Luis
Ermita
Guantánamo
✪ SANTIAGO DE CUBA
Caimanera
Siboney

U.S. NAVAL BASE

Caribbean Sea

0   20   40 miles
0   30   60 kilometers

tion between the Rebel Army combatants and the exploited, landless peasants and agricultural workers of the region. We see the ways in which they transformed each other and together became a stronger, more conscious revolutionary force." Fidel pointed out that once they had eight men and seven rifles in the mountains, victory was in sight. Unity is the source of our strength. Interaction opens the way for the formation of new human beings, one of the main guidelines of revolutionary work. For women this process meant, in practice, a personal revolution: revolutionizing their thinking and actions, leading them to fight the customs of the past, to fight what had seemed time-honored and accepted knowledge.

Mary-Alice correctly highlights Fidel's leadership in the struggle for equality. He called it a revolution because of its scale and scope, the fact that it affects all spheres of social life: production and reproduction.

Finally, I would not want to overlook other elements that add to the book's value, details whose qualities cannot go without mention. First, I found magnificent the quotes from Fidel that appear in boxes, quotes taken from his speeches and other documents on central issues that underlie points touched on in the texts. Another aspect that shows the depth of research that went into the book is the selection that was made of the most appropriate supplementary information. This was done by citing the classics—Marx, Engels, and Lenin—as well as Ana Betancourt, José Antonio Echeverría, Ernesto Che Guevara, Raúl Castro Ruz, José Ramón Machado Ventura, and others.[3]

---

3. **Ana Betancourt** participated in Cuba's first war of independence against Spain, 1868–78. **José Antonio Echeverría** was president of

VERDE OLIVO

GRANMA

In the years after the 1959 victory, said Asela de los Santos, "women stepped out from their traditional duties as homemakers, mothers, and wives. This laid the basis for the big, complex battle for women's full equality."

Inset: Women training as emergency medical aides learn how to tape broken arm, late 1960. The FMC organized Emergency Response Brigades for women who wanted to take an active part in defense against US-backed mercenaries. **Above:** Havana, September 1968, Fidel Castro reviews graduates of first class of 196 women tractor drivers, known as "Las Piccolinas" after nickname for small Italian tractors they operated.

This aspect of the book, read by itself, forms an integral whole that clearly explains Fidel's thesis of the revolution of women within the socialist revolution. A similar exercise can be done with the display quotes taken from the interviews, as well as the photo inserts. These attractive and eloquent elements are deliberately intended to highlight the fundamental concepts expressed in the book. Another detail is the footnotes and glossary, which provide a level of information that must be highlighted.

I left for last the cover, which has an evocative photo by [Raúl] Corrales along with other elements that accurately declare the content of the book. The ordinary women and men we see in the photo, department store workers, as made clear by their dresses, and factory workers, rifle to shoulder, marching resolutely, reflect the image of that historic moment and tell us, half a century later: from the workplace to the trench, defense and work, the reason for living and maintaining, yesterday, today and tomorrow, our socialist revolution.

I want to give thanks on behalf of those who were interviewed—I'm sure Vilma would have liked this book—on behalf of Yolanda, who shares the judgments expressed today, and of the Federation of Cuban Women, to Mary-Alice

---

the Federation of University Students and the principal leader of the Revolutionary Directorate. He was killed in 1957 by henchmen of the Batista dictatorship during an attack on the Presidential Palace. **Ernesto Che Guevara** was an Argentine-born leader of the Cuban Revolution, holding major responsibilities in the revolutionary government. He led Cuban internationalist volunteer detachments in the Congo in 1965 and in Bolivia in 1966–67, where he was murdered by the Bolivian army during a CIA-organized operation. **José Ramón Machado Ventura** is first vice president of Cuba's Council of Ministers and Council of State and second secretary of the Communist Party.

Primary schools abandoned by dictatorship were reopened by the Rebel Army for peasant children and families. **Above:** One of more than 400 schools created in 1958 in the territory of the Second Eastern Front, under the command of Raúl Castro.

"The efforts we made in the Second Front to teach people how to read," said Asela de los Santos, "were a forerunner of the great revolution in education we launched after the victory of January 1959."

and all those who worked with her, and to Pathfinder, for this book we are presenting today. It underscores our unbreakable friendship and our determination to remain united, working for the revolution, here in Cuba and there in the United States.

Thank you very much.

'Our legacy for new generations'

LEIRA SÁNCHEZ

I'D LIKE TO SHARE with you some of the thoughts I had while preparing for this, my first presentation of a book. We began discussing the book at a meeting with the publisher, Pathfinder, in December 2011, when it was still in the final stages of production. We talked about stories and accounts in it that I could relate to, since I'm a teacher myself, and since I have very close relatives who have visited the Second Front.

I expressed in advance my gratitude to Pathfinder for having shown through its pages not only the part women have taken in the revolution but also—and in rich detail—the history of the revolution itself. By presenting this through the words of compañeras Asela, Vilma, and Yolanda, you have enabled us to retrace the history of how our revolution was made along a path that increasingly incorporated women as full participants.

The book's lively presentation makes it highly accessible to young people. It's very valuable for us to be receiving this information from individuals who are among us every

Leira Sánchez is a member of the National Bureau of the Union of Young Communists, responsible for international relations.

day, who continue to make the revolution. It's an important contribution to the new generations. It shows that our people are full of men and women who have helped forge the revolution, and that we have not always been able to write fully about the extent of what we have carried out over the last fifty-four years.

In the course of reading the book, I realized that the photos by themselves conveyed its essence. It's a book that speaks to us in images as well as in words, with great clarity and precision.

I would like to express my gratitude to the publisher for the efforts to record in writing the history of the creation of the Federation of Cuban Women, for chronicling our historical legacy for the new generations of Cubans.

I express my appreciation to the federation for the opportunity not only to read the book, but to share with you how much it meant to me both personally and in my work as a representative of the leadership of the youth organization.

And I'm also grateful to the federation and to Pathfinder for having given me the opportunity once more to hear Asela de los Santos. I met her many years ago when she came to the Enrique José Varona Teachers Institute of the University of Havana, where I was studying. She explained what had been achieved in the Second Front in bringing to life the guiding program outlined by Fidel in *History Will Absolve Me*. It was a history that was virtually unknown to me at that time— I was still very young. What she has been able to communicate to us from that moment up until today is very important.

We, the youth, share the federation's goal of making known this history that has been made by people who acted not with thought to glory but simply to fulfill the commitment they had made.

The fight for women's equality: 'A moral necessity, a revolutionary necessity'

MARY-ALICE WATERS

THANK YOU ARELYS for that warm introduction. Before anything else, I want to extend a very special welcome to Vice President José Ramón Fernández, compañero Armando Hart, General Teté Puebla, and compañero Víctor Dreke. We're honored by their presence, and by the participation of dozens of other revolutionary combatants, too numerous to mention.

For us, it is a real pleasure to be here with so many compañeros and compañeras with whom we have had the privilege of working in recent years, and many others we are only now coming to know.

On behalf of all of us at Pathfinder, I want to express our appreciation to the national leaderships of the Federation of Cuban Women and of the Association of Combatants of the Cuban Revolution, and above all to compañeras Asela de los Santos and Yolanda Ferrer. Without their hard work, and unstinting support, this book—an accurate ex-

---

Mary-Alice Waters is president of Pathfinder Press and a member of the National Committee of the Socialist Workers Party.

pression of a historical truth, of an unwavering political trajectory—would never have become a reality.

From the beginning, the labor and collaboration of three other compañeras who are here today has also been indispensable: Carolina Aguilar, Isabel Moya, and Iraida Aguirrechu.[1] All I can say to each of them is a heartfelt "thank you."

◆

Others on the panel this morning are speaking about what this book represents to so many here in Cuba. I want to say a few words about why Pathfinder Press has published it. About why it is important in the United States and elsewhere outside Cuba to the increasing numbers of workers who are searching for ways to effectively resist, and end, intensifying assaults by the capitalist owners of the means of production and their government on the dignity, wages, job conditions, and rights of working people.

The most succinct answer to why we publish books like the one we are presenting today is that the living example of the men and women who made the Cuban Revolution, and are still making it, needs to be known—because working people everywhere, sooner or later, are being pushed toward revolutionary action.

The accurate record of the Cuban Revolution, told by those who lived it, explaining in their own words why they acted as they did, is indispensable to the revolutionary continuity of the working class. It is part of that continuity, stretching back through the Bolshevik Revolution

1. For information identifying the individuals in the audience mentioned here, see p. 9.

"The example of the Cuban Revolution needs to be known," said Mary-Alice Waters, **"because working people everywhere, sooner or later, are being pushed toward revolutionary action."**

Above: Cops attack dockworkers during protest in Port of Longview, Washington, against lockout and union-busting drive, September 2011. Eight-month battle forced bosses to retreat. **Below:** Rock drillers at Lonmin platinum mine in South Africa celebrate victory in five-week strike despite vicious police assaults that killed 34 miners, September 2012.

of October 1917, to the Paris Commune of 1871, and the Communist Manifesto, which spoke on behalf of the proletariat and its allies in the massive revolutionary upheavals that swept Europe in 1848–49.

Without the real record of the Cuban Revolution being available, in writing, so others can study and know it, future generations will pay a much greater price than necessary in the coming battles whose initial skirmishes are already being fought. That is what is happening today as the opening stages of capitalism's deepening crisis continue to slowly but surely unfold.

◆

The introduction to *The Making of a Revolution Within the Revolution* opens with the statement that this "is not a book about women. Or perhaps it would be more accurate to say that it does not start with women, nor could it. This is a book about the Cuban Revolution . . . about the millions of working people—men and women, of all ages—who have made that socialist revolution, and how their actions transformed them as they fought to transform their world."

One of the most revolutionary lessons recounted in the pages of this new book is Vilma Espín's explanation that as the FMC was being born, those who helped lead it and the women involved in it had "no preconceived structure or agenda."

The organizational structures grew out of the goals—and above all were the product of deeds leading to the accomplishment of those goals. The forms grew out of the participation of more and more women and men in the deepening struggle. First and foremost, women wanted to be involved in a genuine revolution. In the very midst of their efforts, they created a means to that end.

That explanation by Vilma became more and more concrete as work on this book advanced. It brought to life the words of the Communist Manifesto. That the political views of communists "are in no way based on ideas or principles that have been invented, or discovered, by this or that would-be universal reformer. They merely express, in general terms, actual relations springing from an existing class struggle, from a historical movement going on under our very eyes."[2]

The FMC was the product of a very real "existing class struggle." It embodied the proletarian course of the leadership of that struggle—of Fidel above all, but not only Fidel.

◆

"When a deepgoing revolution takes place, women, who have been oppressed for centuries, for millennia, want to take part," says Asela in the interview. Yes! For sure. But she adds another comment a little later that made me stop and think.

In those days, she said, "Change was in the air."

The Cuban Revolution is distinguished from all previous revolutions since the beginning of the modern working-class movement—among other things—by the number of women who became central to its day-to-day leadership. That fact is a registration of the social and economic changes—historic changes—that were gestating in Cuba and elsewhere.

2. Karl Marx, Frederick Engels, *The Communist Manifesto* (Pathfinder, 1970, 1987, 2008), p. 47 [2013 printing].

It is not the caliber of the leadership alone that accounts for the place of women in the revolutionary struggle here in Cuba. Lenin—not to mention Marx and Engels—was no less a champion of women's participation and women's emancipation than Fidel. But objective conditions gave the October Revolution a different set of challenges. It was led to victory by the Bolsheviks at a different moment in history. To return to Asela's phrase, the changes that were in the air in Cuba in the early 1950s had roots in the economic and social convulsions of the second interimperialist slaughter and the other wars that were part of what we know as World War II.

This was brought home to me more than a decade ago in an interview with General Enrique Carreras that is published by Pathfinder in *Making History,* a jewel of a book that also includes insightful interviews with Generals Néstor López Cuba, Harry Villegas, and José Ramón Fernández.

Carreras talks about some of the things that had an impact on him when he was sent to a US Army Air Corps base in San Antonio, Texas, for flight training in 1944. "At Kelly Field," he says, "I saw women training as pilots and gunners for ferrying B-25 bombers from bases in the United States to Canada, and sometimes even to Britain." And Carreras goes on, "I had never before seen women occupying posts previously held only by men, or training alongside men." Here in Cuba at the time, he noted, there was still a lot of machismo. "We did not want to see women in the streets alone going to the store, much less working outside the home, even in the fields."[3]

---

3. *Making History: Interviews with Four Generals of Cuba's Revolutionary Armed Forces* (Pathfinder, 1999), p. 67 [2015 printing].

But with the revolution, Carreras concludes, that all began to be uprooted.

Yolanda sums it up well in these pages. "From the first day of the revolution," she says, "what it meant to be female began to change." Prejudice "began to lose ground." It didn't end all of a sudden, but it palpably lost more and more space. Women learned, and proved, that they—together with men who were revolutionary—were capable of doing whatever was necessary.

◆

The birth of the FMC and its character can only be understood as a front within the revolution. Not as something outside it. Not as a phenomenon parallel to it.

The fight for women's participation in the Cuban Revolution did not open on January 1, 1959, however. It began with political preparations for the assault on Moncada itself and the insistence by Fidel and Abel, as well as Haydée and Melba, that women would be among the combatants.[4] The advances for women continued in the clandestine struggle, not only in Santiago but across the country, and in the Rebel Army. And that is what this book brings to life.

---

4. On July 26, 1953, one hundred sixty revolutionaries under the command of Fidel Castro launched simultaneous insurrectionary attacks on the Moncada army garrison in Santiago de Cuba and on the garrison in Bayamo. After the attacks' failure, Batista's forces brutally tortured and massacred fifty-six captured revolutionaries, including Abel Santamaría, who was second in command. Haydée Santamaría (sister of Abel) and Melba Hernández were the two female combatants. After the July 26 assault, Haydée and Melba were captured and imprisoned for seven months. A broad national amnesty campaign won release of the others in May 1955.

"The fight for women's participation in the revolution began with political preparations for the 1953 assault on Moncada garrison and the insistence by Fidel Castro, as well as others, that women would be among the combatants," **said Waters.**

Above: Melba Hernández and Haydée Santamaría (third and fourth from left) leave Guanajay women's prison, February 1954, after serving seven-month sentences for their participation in that action, which opened the revolutionary struggle to overthrow the Batista dictatorship.

Carolina Aguilar once commented in a discussion that the FMC was born with the formation of the Mariana Grajales Platoon. It's a striking image, one also captured in Fidel's statement some thirty years later that the decision to send Women's Antiaircraft Artillery Regiments to Angola in 1988 was not a military necessity. It was—and I'm quoting Fidel—"a moral necessity, a revolutionary necessity."[5]

The revolutionary course that led from Moncada to the Mariana Grajales Platoon, the FMC, and the Women's Antiaircraft Artillery Regiments has never faltered, not from July 26, 1953, to today.

General Teté Puebla—in her book *Marianas in Combat*—relates the facts about Fidel naming her director of the Guaicanamar Cattle Plan in Jaruco in 1969, in order to show that women as well as men could lead. That a woman was a candidate to head up any front, carry out any task of the revolution. One of her jobs, she said, was to get women from peasant families involved in agricultural work.

When Fidel took her to Jaruco, the men there said they wouldn't work with her, Teté explains. "She might be a captain, they said, but she's not working with me. I won't work with women." But that began to change in barely a month, as she showed she could work as hard as any man—and harder than many.[6]

In the United States with the rise of the women's move-

5. Quoted in *The Making of a Revolution*, p. 35.

6. See Teté Puebla, *Marianas in Combat: Teté Puebla and the Mariana Grajales Women's Platoon in Cuba's Revolutionary War, 1956–58* (Pathfinder, 2003), p. 75 [2016 printing]. The platoon, organized in September 1958, was the first combat unit in the Rebel Army composed of women.

ment in the late 1960s and early 1970s—part of the broad radicalization that was a response, above all, to the mass struggle for Black rights and opposition to the US rulers' war against the people of Vietnam—there was a popular tee shirt that I enjoyed wearing on appropriate occasions. It bore the slogan, "A woman must do any job twice as well as a man in order to be considered half as good." That was the mission Fidel gave Teté. And she fulfilled it.

For those of us outside Cuba, and those of younger generations here who did not live the Cuban Revolution from the inside, these accounts by Carreras and Teté are not "stories." They give us the concrete richness and detail of the experiences that allow us to understand what the revolution within the revolution meant. To understand the political battles that determined the life or death of the revolution.

It is the only way those who seek to emulate the example of Cuba, now and in the future, can learn from the record of your setbacks as well as from your victories.

◆

I want to end by emphasizing what for revolutionists is probably Asela's most important contribution in the pages of *Making a Revolution Within the Revolution*. That is the clarity and sharpness with which she has sketched the accelerating social revolution led by the Rebel Army in the area of the Second Front in the last months of the war.

It's not that this aspect of the revolution was previously unknown. Nor, of course, was the deepening social revolution in enormous areas of Cuba's eastern-most province limited to the Second Front. In *La victoria estratégica* [Strategic victory], for example, Fidel has a few words—far too few—about the emerging governmental body established at the La Plata Headquarters of the Rebel Army in September 1958. The Civil Administration of the Free Territory "took responsibility," he says, "for necessary aspects of economic and social life in the rebel mountains, a vast territory that had been definitively liberated, whose population lacked almost everything."

Fidel calls it "the embryo of the new state that would emerge after the revolutionary triumph, a state faithful to the democratic and popular spirit of the revolution."[7]

But Asela's sketch of the veritable 'republic in arms' established, under the leadership of the Rebel Army, by peasants and workers in the territory of the Second Front is drawn in richer detail than in any other book I know of available outside Cuba. In her brief account of the policies implemented by that revolutionary power, under the command of Raúl, we see the whole future course of the revolution. In a few short months, they drew layer upon layer of the toilers into initiating land reform, opening more than 400 schools, organizing the first literacy campaign, establishing clinics and field hospitals, building roads, printing educational materials, collecting taxes from the big produc-

7. Fidel Castro, *La victoria estratégica: Por todos los caminos de la Sierra* [Strategic victory: Along every road in the Sierra] (Havana: Publications Office of the Council of State, 2010), pp. 363–64. *La victoria estratégica* is the first of two volumes by Fidel Castro, both published since 2010, recounting the Rebel Army's summer 1958 defeat of the Batista dictatorship's "final offensive" and then the revolutionaries' counteroffensive to extend the struggle to the rest of Cuba, culminating in the victorious general strike and popular insurrection of January 1, 1959. The second volume is entitled *La contraofensiva estratégica: De la Sierra Maestra a Santiago de Cuba* [Strategic counteroffensive: From the Sierra Maestra to Santiago de Cuba].

ers, establishing universal protection of the toilers under a rule of law—and more.

◈

Finally, I want to speak of the more than one hundred photos that provide a pictorial summary of the most important elements of the history recounted in the pages of *The Making of a Revolution Within the Revolution.* We've learned over time at Pathfinder that the work that goes into putting together these photo pages makes a significant difference, especially to new readers—workers, farmers, and youth— for whom this is all unknown. That wealth of photos, and the display quotes and captions drawn from the interviews themselves, give new readers a way into the book. It is, we could say, a small but faithful revolutionary "picture book within the book."

We received a great deal of help from a broad number of compañeras and compañeros here, without which this vital component of the book would have been impossible. Help in finding photos, identifying individuals, confirming dates, locations, and other details, securing the best quality reproductions possible, and much more. Comrades from *Bohemia* and *Granma* and many individuals were part of this, but our special appreciation goes to the family of Raúl Corrales; and to the Council of State Office of Historical Affairs, director Eugenio Suárez and Elsa Montero, organizer of the photo archive, in particular. Both the Office of Historical Affairs and the Corrales family authorized the use of many photos in this edition free of charge. And that includes the cover photo taken by Raúl Corrales.

Nothing could capture the political power of this book

more eloquently than that striking image of the militia unit of department store clerks who were women, marching together with brewery workers on May Day 1959—with pride, confidence, determination, and discipline (discipline from inside, discipline internalized from and for struggle) marking every line of their faces and demeanor.

For all this, we can only say to you, "Gracias."

'Without dogma, schemas, or jargon'

MARY-ALICE WATERS

The phenomenon of women's participation in the revolution is a revolution within another revolution. If I were asked what is the most revolutionary thing the revolution is doing, I would answer that it is precisely this—the revolution that is occurring among the women of our country.

FIDEL CASTRO
December 9, 1966

True equality between men and women can become a reality only when the exploitation of both by capital has been abolished, and private work in the home has been transformed into a public industry.

FREDERICK ENGELS
July 5, 1885

The Making of a Revolution Within the Revolution is not a book about women. Or perhaps it would be more accurate to say that it does not start with women, nor could it. This

---

Introduction to *Women in Cuba: The Making of a Revolution Within the Revolution.*

is a book about the Cuban Revolution. It is about the millions of working people—men and women, of all ages—who have made that socialist revolution, and how their actions transformed them as they fought to transform their world. We had "no preconceived structure or agenda," Vilma Espín says here. There was "just a desire by women . . . to participate in a revolutionary process, whose aim was to transform the lives of those who had been exploited and discriminated against and create a better society for all." And the leadership of the revolution responded.

Espín was a legendary combatant of the July 26 Movement in the Santiago de Cuba underground and the Rebel Army's Second Front during the revolutionary war and mass popular struggle of the 1950s that brought down the bloody military dictatorship of Fulgencio Batista. Following the January 1, 1959, victory, she became the central leader of the ongoing revolutionary activity that gave birth to the Federation of Cuban Women (FMC), serving as its president until her death in 2007.

The Cuban Revolution began long before victorious Rebel Army columns entered Santiago de Cuba, Santa Clara, and Havana in the opening days of January 1959, propelled by popular insurrections and a mass general strike that swept the country.

It begins with the vanguard of men and women who came together in the wake of Batista's March 10, 1952, coup, determined to oppose it at all costs. It begins with their unconditional rejection of a political system marked by decades of rampant corruption and subordination to the dictates of the Yankee imperialist colossus to the north. It begins with a determination to reknit the continuity of Cuba's long history of struggle for national sovereignty, independence, and deepgoing social reform.

The course of the revolution goes through the July 26, 1953, assaults on the Moncada army garrison in Santiago de Cuba and the Carlos Manuel de Céspedes barracks in Bayamo, led by Fidel Castro and Abel Santamaría, the actions that marked the opening of the revolutionary struggle. It proceeds through the years of patient work organizing a broad mass campaign for amnesty for the jailed combatants from the assault on Moncada and other political prisoners. It encompasses the nationwide effort to spread the popular revolutionary program presented by Castro in *History Will Absolve Me*, his courtroom defense of the Moncada fighters, which became the foundation of the July 26 Movement.

The channel of the revolution flows through the *Granma* expedition, which launched the revolutionary war at the end of 1956. Through the actions of the fledgling Rebel Army, as it consolidated support among the rural toilers of the Sierra Maestra mountains and other parts of eastern Cuba throughout 1957–58. Through its actions as it began to lead in practice toward the new economic and social relations that working people would soon create across the country.

The thread of that history, broadly known inside Cuba and elsewhere, runs through this book. What emerges with new sharpness and clarity in these pages is something that is less well-known. It is a picture of the *social revolution* led by the Rebel Army in the Sierras during the two years of the revolutionary war, and how that revolution prepared and educated those who were touched by it.

In the firsthand accounts of Asela de los Santos and Vilma Espín, we see the interaction between the Rebel Army combatants and the exploited, landless peasants and agricultural workers of the region. We see the ways in which

"Vilma Espín was a legendary combatant in the Rebel Army and, after the January 1959 victory, became the central leader of the Federation of Cuban Women," said Waters.

Above: First leadership meeting of July 26 Movement held in Sierra Maestra, February 1957. Among participants were (from left), *Granma* expeditionary Ciro Redondo, Vilma Espín, Fidel Castro, Haydée Santamaría, Celia Sánchez. Espín and Sánchez, working with Frank País, organized urban recruitment and supply network for Rebel Army. **Below:** Fidel Castro, Celia Sánchez (center), and Espín at FMC founding, August 1960.

they transform each other and together become a stronger, more conscious revolutionary force.

Through these accounts, we see the growing trust the Rebel Army wins among the rural poor, who are treated for the first time ever with respect and dignity. We see how the proletarian army-in-becoming responds to that trust, becoming ever more confident, clear-sighted, and class conscious as they fight together to expand education and health care and fulfill other long-cherished dreams of the toilers, even in the midst of a war. And we see the growing involvement of women, in the ranks and in the leadership.

The Rebel Army's defeat of the Batista regime's wishfully mislabeled "encircle and annihilate" operations, after three months of battle in mid-1958, opened the way for the rebels' strategic military counteroffensive, leading to the rout and collapse of the tyranny a few months later. The recent publication of Fidel Castro's two-volume account of the Rebel Army's actions from May through December 1958—*La victoria estratégica* and *La contraofensiva estratégica*—makes an understanding of those crucial months of the revolutionary war more accessible than ever before.[1]

The withdrawal of Batista's battered ground troops from large swaths of the mountainous regions of Cuba's Oriente province—stretching north and east of Santiago de Cuba toward Guantánamo, Baracoa, and beyond—gave the revolutionary forces the necessary time and space to consolidate what was known as the Frank País Second Eastern Front. Deadly bombing raids and strafing runs by Batista's air force continued throughout the region, which was con-

---

1. See footnote, p. 43

trolled by the Rebel Army forces commanded by Raúl Castro. But in those closing months of the revolutionary war, the enemy's largely demoralized foot soldiers ventured from their barracks less and less.

With broad popular support, the Rebel Army's incipient government-in-arms increasingly displaced the crumbling structures of the capitalist regime in the region, as they organized working people to take charge of health care and education, justice, agriculture, construction, communications, taxation, and established their own radio station and other means of providing news and orientation. The toilers within the Second Front began to implement the program outlined in *History Will Absolve Me*.

It became a "virtual republic," as Vilma Espín affirms here. And one with a new class character.

A congress of peasants in arms was organized by the Rebel Army in September 1958, land reform was codified by military decree in the liberated territories, and titles were issued to those who worked the land.

More than four hundred primary schools were opened, organized by the Rebel Army's department of education headed by Asela de los Santos, as peasant families enthusiastically carried out a census of the children, searched for suitable classrooms, found books, and built desks and benches. Night-time classes for combatants often used the same premises.

Clinics and field hospitals were established, treating combatants, including wounded enemy soldiers, and local residents alike. They provided the first medical care most peasants had ever received.

With the participation of all, roads were repaired and new ones opened.

"In the firsthand accounts of Asela de los Santos and Vilma Espín," said Mary-Alice Waters, **"we see the interaction between the Rebel Army combatants and the exploited, landless peasants and agricultural workers of the region. We see the ways in which they transform each other and together become a stronger, more conscious revolutionary force."**

Above: Field hospital near Fidel Castro's Rebel Army headquarters at La Plata, Sierra Maestra, late 1958. Patients included Rebel Army combatants, local peasants, workers and their families, and captured enemy combatants. All were treated on a first-come, first-served basis.

Taxes on output were collected from the owners of sugar mills, mining operations, and coffee plantations. The workers knew exactly how much had been produced and shipped out.

Disputes were settled and marriages celebrated.

A popular revolution, a proletarian revolution-in-becoming, was organized in the mountains of the east, as the workers and peasants mobilized to begin transforming social relations. It spread across Cuba with the victory of January 1, 1959.

◆

"When a deepgoing revolution takes place women, who have been oppressed for millennia, want to take part," Asela de los Santos reminds us here.

The growing participation of women was a seamless part of this revolutionary upheaval. Forged in the heat of popular mobilizations in the opening months of 1959, what became the Federation of Cuban Women grew out of women's determination to participate in the revolution—not the other way around. As Vilma Espín describes, women insisted on organizing themselves, and being organized, into the most pressing tasks of the revolution. In the process they created an organization that would enable them to do just that.

Many years later, a journalist for the Cuban daily *Granma* asked Vilma Espín whether she had anticipated all this when she was fighting in the mountains of eastern Cuba. Had she ever imagined she would be so involved and identified with making—as Fidel Castro called it—a revolution within the revolution? Espín's spontaneous response was:

Never! It hadn't even remotely occurred to me that
a women's organization should exist. I had never
even thought about it. I joined the struggle as part
of a group that included young women and men. It
never occurred to me we'd have to carry out special
work with women. . . .
    When the idea of creating a women's
organization was suggested to me, it came as
a surprise. . . . But soon after it was created I
realized that yes, it was indispensable. . . . It was
an enormous revolutionary force.[2]

Part II of *The Making of a Revolution Within the Revolution* takes us through this "Birth of the Federation of Cuban
Women" in interviews with Vilma Espín and Yolanda Ferrer.

What strikes the reader more than anything else in Espín's account is the absence of dogma or schemas, the absence of clotted political jargon. There was only one guide:
opening the way for the broadest layers of women to become involved—with organization, effectiveness, and discipline—in ongoing struggles and the construction of a
new social order.

In the beginning was the deed. Leaders were those who
led.

"Learn in the morning and teach in the afternoon" became a popular revolutionary slogan, reflecting a fact of
life. Often that meant doing so under fire—literally—as
Washington tried unsuccessfully, over and over, to organize
and arm a counterrevolutionary cadre. As on every other

---

2. Interview with Mirta Rodríguez Calderón, August 1985, in *La mujer
en Cuba* [Women in Cuba] (Havana: Editora Política, 1990), pp. 79–81.

front of the advancing revolution, form followed content, and organizational structures were codified as the struggle permitted.

Nothing captures this better than the image of the school for young women from the countryside, training to staff child care centers, being strafed and bombed by US-based planes a few days prior to the US-organized invasion at the Bay of Pigs in April 1961. "Not a single one asked to go home," Espín notes. "Everyone stayed."

"When I talk about how the federation was created," Espín says here,

> I always emphasize that at the time we didn't talk about women's liberation. We didn't talk about women's emancipation, or the struggle for equality. We didn't use those terms then. What we did talk about was participation. Women wanted to participate. . . .
>
> There was real proof, every day, that the revolution wasn't just hot air, it wasn't empty phrases of the kind people were used to hearing from politicians in the past. This was the genuine thing. And women wanted to be part of it, to *do* something. The more the revolutionary laws strengthened this conviction, the more women demanded a chance to contribute—and the more they saw how necessary their contribution was.

Cuba in the 1950s was one of the more economically developed countries of Latin America, not one of the poorest. Yet only 13.5 percent of women worked outside the home in 1953, many of them without pay. By 1981, barely twenty years after the triumph of the revolution, that figure had risen to 44.5 percent, and by 2008 stood at 59 percent.

In 1953, of those women in the workforce "with or without pay," the largest single category, totaling more than 70,000, were domestic servants, a large proportion of whom were black. That was close to 30 percent of all women who had jobs. Some worked for as little as 20 cents a day or for room and board alone—which could mean a mat to sleep on and leftover food from the plates of their employer.

The social dynamic of the early years of the revolution is dramatically represented by the FMC-organized night schools for former domestic workers, women left with no way to make a living as their well-off employers abandoned the country. Retrained for jobs ranging from taxi drivers and auto mechanics to bank clerks, secretaries, child care workers, and poultry farmers, they began new lives—with confidence and pride.

The same dynamic was central to one of the most extensive FMC campaigns in the first years of the revolution, the establishment of the Ana Betancourt School for young peasant women. Between 1961 and 1963, twenty-one thousand, with their parents' consent, came to Havana for an intensive six-month course during which they learned to read and write, cut and sew, and acquired the foundations of scientific nutrition and hygiene. Some learned basic office-work skills as well.

One of the charges leveled against the Cuban Revolution by its opponents in other countries, often by women who came out of some of the feminist organizations of the 1960s and 70s, is that the FMC, by teaching women how to make clothes for themselves and their families, reinforced traditional female stereotypes. It bolstered women's oppression rather than advancing women's liberation, they claimed. In the *Granma* interview quoted earlier, Espín was asked if she still thought they had done the right thing.

"Yes, I do," was her immediate answer, "because at that time it was what allowed us to draw women out of their homes. It's what made it possible for young women from the Escambray mountains and the Baracoa region, where the counterrevolution was working intensively on peasant families, to come to the capital, learn what the revolution was really about, and become the first cadres of the revolution in those areas.

"This was important, not only in combating the counterrevolution," Espín said, "but in terms of the development of women as cadres. . . . We started from where women were at to raise them to a new level."

The revolution in women's social, economic, and political status was not a phenomenon *parallel* to the revolutionary advance of Cuba's toilers. It took place *within* that advance.

◆

Addressing a leadership meeting of the Federation of Cuban Women in December 1966, Cuban prime minister Fidel Castro called attention to the antiwoman prejudices that prevailed in prerevolutionary Cuba, as throughout class societies the world over. "Prejudices that have existed, not just for decades or centuries," Castro said, "but for millennia." He pointed

> to the belief that all a woman was good for was to scrub dishes, wash, iron, cook, keep house, and bear children—age-old prejudices that placed women in

an inferior position in society. In effect women did not have a productive place in society.

Under capitalism, he went on, the big majority of women are "doubly exploited or doubly humiliated."

> A poor woman, whether a worker or belonging to a working-class family, was exploited simply because of her humbler status, because she was a worker. Moreover, within her own class, as a working woman, she was looked down on and underrated. Not only was she underestimated, exploited, and looked down on by the exploiting classes, but even within her own class she was the object of countless prejudices. . . .
> There are two sectors in this country, two components of society that, aside from economic reasons, have had other motives for sympathizing with and feeling enthusiasm for the revolution: the black population of Cuba and the country's women.[3]

The political clarity and decisive leadership given the fight for women's equality by Fidel Castro, the central leader of the Cuban Revolution for more than half a century, is one of the truest measures of the working-class character of that revolution and the caliber of its leadership. It has been so from the earliest days of the fight against the Batista dictatorship. That same clar-

3. Fidel Castro, Vilma Espín, *Women and the Cuban Revolution* (Pathfinder, 1981), pp. 67–68, 69 [2015 printing].

ity and decisiveness has been a guarantee of the revolutionary alliance of workers and farmers in Cuba over those decades.

At every point in the struggle, women were part of the vanguard and its leadership. Women such as Haydée Santamaría and Melba Hernández, who joined the assault on the Moncada military garrison in Santiago de Cuba on July 26, 1953. Women like Celia Sánchez, the principal organizer of the July 26 Movement in Manzanillo, the first woman to join the Rebel Army as a combatant, and a member of its general staff. Women like Vilma Espín, whose story you will read in the pages to follow.

The Cuban Revolution is distinguished from all previous revolutions in the history of the modern working-class movement, among other things, by the number of women who were central to its day-to-day leadership.

Moreover, the speed of women's economic and social advances in the thirty years between 1960 and 1990—advances measured by education, employment, infant and maternal mortality rates, and other gauges—allowed Cuban women to conquer a degree of equality that it took women in the United States and other industrialized capitalist countries more than a century and a half to achieve.

But none of this was inevitable.

"One of the ways our revolution will be judged in coming years," Fidel Castro told the Second Congress of the FMC in 1974, "is how we have resolved the problems facing women in our society and our country."

Without the clear course charted by Fidel as well as other central leaders—including Abel Santamaría, Frank País, and Raúl Castro, all of whom readers come to know better in the pages of this book—the record of Cuba's revolutionary struggle would have been far less exemplary. Es-pín notes, for example, that Frank País's leadership and "at-titude toward women" is what made it possible for women in the July 26 Movement in Santiago de Cuba "to work as complete equals with men." The political determination of Fidel Castro to challenge the antiwoman prejudices held by some who were among the best cadres of the movement was demonstrated by the fight he waged in 1958 to organize the Mariana Gra-jales Women's Platoon of the Rebel Army—something Es-pín points to as "an extraordinary moment in the history of women's participation in the revolution."

"Some of our comrades were still very machista," Fidel told a June 1988 send-off for a battery of the First Women's Antiaircraft Artillery Regiment of Guantánamo leaving for Angola the next day. The women had volunteered for an internationalist mission, defending newly built airstrips in southern Angola from attack by the air force of the South African apartheid regime. Also invited to that gathering were ambassadors of African countries accredited in Cuba. Fidel continued:

> Some of the men asked "How can you give those rifles to those women when we are unarmed?"
> That reaction really made me mad. So I told one of them: "I'll tell you why we're going to give those rifles to those women: because they're better soldiers than you." I didn't say another word.
> We were living in a class society, a society where women were discriminated against, a society where a revolution had to come about, a revolution in

which women would have to demonstrate their capacity and their merits.

"What was our objective?" Fidel asked.

First, we believed in women's capacity, women's courage, their capacity to fight; and second, we knew that such a precedent would have enormous importance in the future, when the moment came to raise the question of equality in our society.[4]

The combat record of the Mariana Grajales Women's Platoon proved to be one of the most outstanding in the revolutionary war. And the precedent set was never lost.

Addressing the guests from the diplomatic corps attending the send-off for the women's antiaircraft regiment, Castro joked, "Perhaps our guests could be asking themselves this evening if it's necessary for a battery of women to go to southern Angola . . . whether there are no more Cuban men to send over there and we have to resort to sending Cuban women. In truth, that's not the way it is."

The deployment of the women's antiaircraft artillery battery to Angola "is not a military necessity," Fidel told them. "It is a moral necessity, a revolutionary necessity."

What the reader will find in these pages is the consistency of the revolutionary leadership of Cuba on the fight for women's equality over more than half a century. And

---

4. Speech at June 24, 1988, meeting with members of the First Women's Antiaircraft Artillery Regiment of Guantánamo, in *Mujeres y Revolución* [Women and Revolution] (Havana: Editorial de la Mujer, 2006, 2010), pp. 216–17.

its continuity reaching all the way back to Karl Marx and Frederick Engels, founders of the modern working-class movement.

◆

The three authors of this book, who knew each other and worked together over some five decades, reflect two different generations in the leadership of "a revolution within the revolution."

Espín and de los Santos were lifelong friends and co-combatants from their earliest days as students at the University of Oriente in Santiago de Cuba. Following the March 10, 1952, military coup that brought Batista to power, they were among the first to become involved in the struggle against the increasingly brutal US-backed dictatorship. They worked side by side in Santiago's underground and in the Rebel Army's Second Eastern Front. After the 1959 victory, de los Santos joined Espín from 1960 to 1966 in the leadership of the newly formed Federation of Cuban Women, serving as the organization's first general secretary.

Yolanda Ferrer, general secretary of the Federation of Cuban Women today, tells the story of the tremendous leaps made by women in the first years of the revolution from a different perspective. She was part of a new generation, too young to have been involved in the struggle against the dictatorship, that threw itself into the great social battles that pushed forward the revolution. Barely in their teens, these young women joined the first militia units and helped build the communist youth organization. They formed the core of the historic countrywide campaign that in 1961, in a single year-long mobilization, wiped out illiteracy among the adult population of Cuba—23 percent of whom, the majority women, had never had the opportunity to learn to read or write.

It was the intertwining of these two generations in the tasks of the revolution that assured the energy and discipline of the campaigns that marked the character of the FMC at its birth. In the accounts of the three authors we see—firsthand—the impact of the revolutionary struggles that transformed them along with millions of other Cuban women, as they fought to build a society in which, as Frederick Engels expressed it more than a hundred and twenty-five years ago, exploitation by capital has been abolished and "true equality between men and women can become a reality." If the struggle continues.

◆

The Making of a Revolution Within the Revolution would not have been possible without the extensive collaboration provided by the leadership of the Federation of Cuban Women over a number of years, including the help of its cadres in cities from Havana to Santiago de Cuba and Holguín.

Special thanks is due above all to FMC general secretary Yolanda Ferrer and to Asela de los Santos for the many hours they devoted to reading drafts, correcting errors, and explaining aspects of the history of the Cuban Revolution that would have otherwise remained obscure.

Carolina Aguilar, one of the founding cadres and long-time leaders of the FMC, and Isabel Moya, director of Editorial de la Mujer, the FMC's publishing house, offered their time, suggestions, collaboration, and encouragement at every turn, including the scouring of archives for photos, documents, and long-out-of-print sources.

Iraida Aguirrechu, senior editor at Editora Política, the publishing house of the Central Committee of the Communist Party of Cuba, provided unstinting support, help, and editorial expertise, as always.

The Office of Historical Affairs of the Council of State, through its director, Eugenio Suárez, and Elsa Montero, organizer of the photographic archive (and herself a Rebel Army messenger at fourteen and combatant in the Third Front under the command of Juan Almeida), provided invaluable assistance, making available numerous historic photos reproduced in this book and identifying individuals, locations, dates, and circumstances of many others.

Directors of the archives at *Bohemia* and *Granma*, Magaly Miranda Martínez and Alejandro Debén, were generous in the time they made available to aid in the search for many other photos capturing specific moments and events in the history of the revolution.

Last but far from least, we express appreciation to the family of photographer Raúl Corrales for allowing reproduction, free of cost in this edition, not only of three photographs that are reproduced inside the book, but the evocative photo of a workers' militia unit that appears on the cover.

The armed women department store employees in their white-dress workclothes—marching side by side on May 1, 1959, with their compañero brewery workers, each ready to give her or his life to defend their revolution—captures an indelible image of the vanguard of the Cuban working class at that decisive moment in the class struggle. It does so with an insight that few photographers other than Raúl Corrales ever achieved.

Department store salesperson was one of the few jobs

deemed appropriate for a woman in Cuba in the 1950s. And there was good reason for them to be armed. Two of the most destructive actions of the counterrevolution were the fire-bombings of two famous department stores in central Havana, El Encanto and La Epoca. A militia member on guard duty that night, a woman like those on the cover of this book, died as she rushed back into the inferno of El Encanto to try to retrieve funds the workers had collected to build a child care center there. In 1960–61 alone, nine Havana department stores were the targets of such attacks.

The Making of a Revolution Within the Revolution is dedicated to the new generations of women and men, in Cuba and worldwide, for whom the accurate history of the Cuban Revolution and how it was made is, and will be, an indispensable armament in the tumultuous class battles whose initial skirmishes are already upon us.

JANUARY 2012

WOMEN'S EMANCIPATION AND THE WORKING CLASS

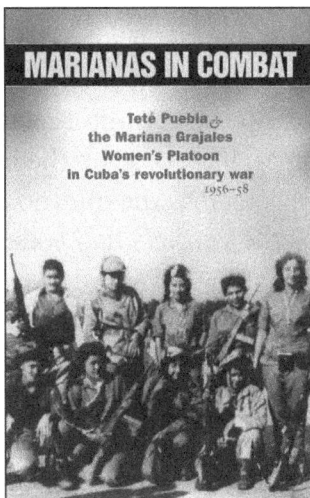

Marianas in Combat

Teté Puebla and the
Mariana Grajales Women's Platoon
in Cuba's Revolutionary War 1956-58

TETÉ PUEBLA

Brigadier General Teté Puebla, the highest-ranking woman in Cuba's Revolutionary Armed Forces, joined the struggle to overthrow the US-backed dictatorship of Fulgencio Batista in 1956. She was fifteen years old. This is her story— from clandestine action in the cities, to serving as an officer in the victorious Rebel Army's first all-women's unit. $10. Also in Spanish and Farsi.

New Expanded Edition!
Cosmetics, Fashion, and the Exploitation of Women

MARY-ALICE WATERS
JOSEPH HANSEN, EVELYN REED

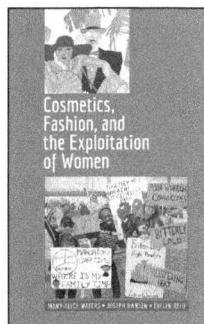

"Norms of beauty and fashion are inseparable from the class struggle." That's the title of the opening chapter of this timely new edition of a lively 1950s debate in the *Militant*, a socialist newsweekly. How cosmetics and fashion monopolies rake in profits from social insecurities of women and adolescents. Why women's integration into the workforce and unions is a major advance in the fight for emancipation. A Marxist classic on the origins of women's oppression and the working-class road forward. $15. Also in Spanish, French, Farsi, Greek.

Women's Liberation and the African Freedom Struggle

THOMAS SANKARA

"There is no true social revolution without the liberation of women," explains the leader of the 1983–87 revolution in the West African country of Burkina Faso. $5. Also in Spanish, French, Farsi, Arabic.

CUBA'S SOCIALIST REVOLUTION AND THE WORLD

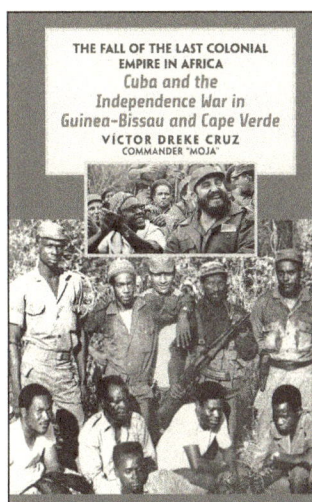

New!
Cuba and the Independence War in Guinea-Bissau and Cape Verde

The Fall of the Last Colonial Empire in Africa

VÍCTOR DREKE

In 1974–75 the people of two West African countries, Guinea-Bissau and Cape Verde, put an end to 500 years of Portuguese colonial exploitation. Led by a popular movement forged by Amílcar Cabral, their struggle triggered the collapse of Portugal's entire colonial empire and brought down the 40-year fascist dictatorship in Portugal itself. Víctor Dreke's firsthand account brings to life this decisive victory. $7. Also in Spanish.

Cuba and the Coming American Revolution

JACK BARNES

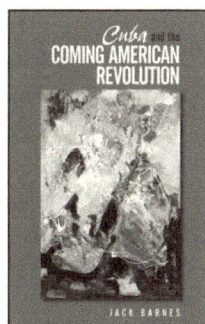

This is a book about the example set by the Cuban people that socialist revolution is not only necessary—it can be made. A book about the struggles of workers and other exploited producers in the imperialist heartland, and the youth attracted to them. About the class struggle in the US, where the revolutionary capacities of working people are as utterly discounted by the ruling powers as were those of the Cuban toilers. $10. Also in Spanish, French, Farsi.

'Cuba Will Never Adopt Capitalist Methods'

FIDEL CASTRO

Cuba's rectification process, its contributions to building socialism worldwide, and the victory of Cuban-Angolan-SWAPO forces against the South African army in southern Angola in early 1988. $5

CAPITALIST CRISIS AND THE FIGHT FOR WORKERS POWER

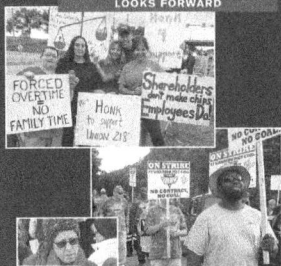

The Low Point of Labor Resistance Is Behind Us

The Socialist Workers Party Looks Forward

JACK BARNES
MARY-ALICE WATERS
STEVE CLARK

The global order imposed by Washington is shattering. A long retreat by the working class and unions has come to an end. The bosses and their government are stepping up attacks on our wages, conditions, and constitutional rights. This book highlights opportunities for building a mass proletarian party able to lead the struggle to end capitalist rule, opening a socialist future for humanity. $10. Also in Spanish, French, Greek.

Malcolm X, Black Liberation, and the Road to Workers Power

JACK BARNES

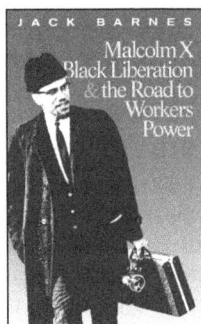

"The conquest of state power by a class-conscious vanguard of the working class is the mightiest weapon possible in the fight against Black oppression, the subjugation of women, Jew-hatred, and every form of human degradation inherited from class society." $20. Also in Spanish, French, Farsi, Arabic, Greek.

Teamster Rebellion

FARRELL DOBBS

The 1934 strikes that won union recognition for truckers and warehouse workers in Minneapolis and helped pave the way for the working-class social movement that built the industrial unions. The first of four volumes by a central leader of these battles and of the Socialist Workers Party. $16. Also in Spanish, French, Farsi, Greek.

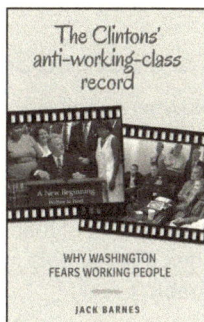

EXPAND YOUR
REVOLUTIONARY LIBRARY

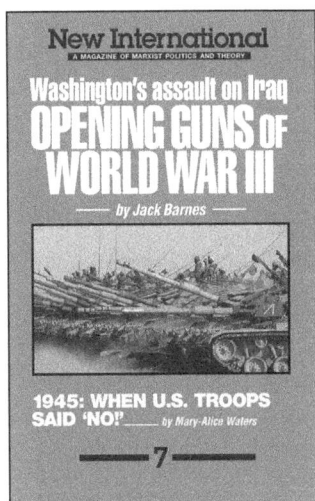

Opening Guns of World War III: Washington's Assault on Iraq

JACK BARNES

The murderous assault on Iraq in 1990–91 heralded increasingly sharp conflicts among imperialist powers, growing instability of capitalism, and more wars. Also includes:

1945: When US Troops Said 'No!' by Mary-Alice Waters
Lessons from the Iran-Iraq War by Samad Sharif

In *New International* no. 7. $14. Also in Spanish, French, Farsi.

U.S. Imperialism Has Lost the Cold War

JACK BARNES

The collapse of regimes across Eastern Europe and the USSR claiming to be communist did not mean workers and farmers there had been crushed. In today's sharpening class conflicts and wars, these toilers are joining working people the world over in the class struggle against capitalist exploitation. In *New International* no. 11. $14. Also in Spanish, French, Farsi, Greek.

The First and Second Delarations of Havana

Nowhere are the questions of revolutionary strategy that today confront men and women on the front lines of struggles in the Americas addressed with greater truthfulness and clarity than in these uncompromising indictments of imperialist plunder and "the exploitation of man by man." Adopted by million-strong assemblies of the Cuban people in 1960 and 1962. $10. Also in Spanish, French, Farsi, Arabic, Greek.

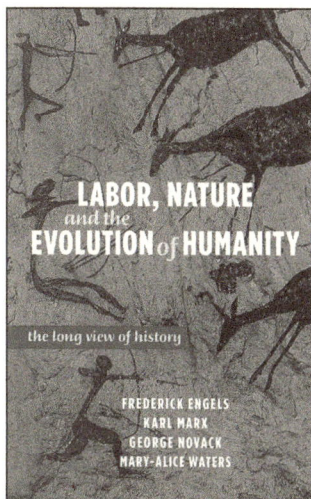

Labor, Nature, and the Evolution of Humanity

The Long View of History

FREDERICK ENGELS, KARL MARX
GEORGE NOVACK
MARY-ALICE WATERS

Without understanding that social labor, transforming nature, has driven humanity's evolution for millions of years, working people are unable to see beyond the capitalist epoch of class exploitation that warps all human relations, ideas, and values. $12. Also in Spanish and French.

Panama: The Truth About the U.S. Invasion

CINDY JAQUITH, DON ROJAS, FIDEL CASTRO

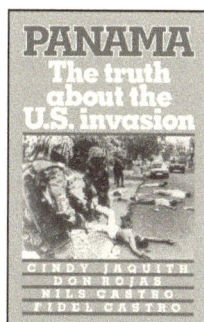

Washington's probes to retake control of the Panama Canal and broader military operations in the Americas are good reason to recall the invasion of Panama in 1989, at the time the biggest US military action since Vietnam. A threat to the sovereignty of every nation in Latin America, these moves mark US imperialism's determination to crush the example set by Cuba's socialist revolution. Includes speech by Fidel Castro. $5

Puerto Rico: Independence Is a Necessity

RAFAEL CANCEL MIRANDA

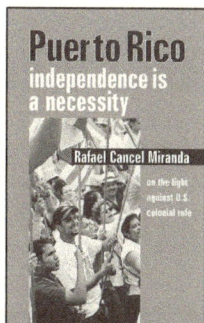

One of the five Puerto Rican Nationalists imprisoned by Washington for more than 25 years and released in 1979 speaks out on the brutal reality of US colonial domination, the example of Cuba's socialist revolution, and the ongoing struggle for independence. $5. Also in Spanish and Farsi.

PATHFINDER AROUND THE WORLD

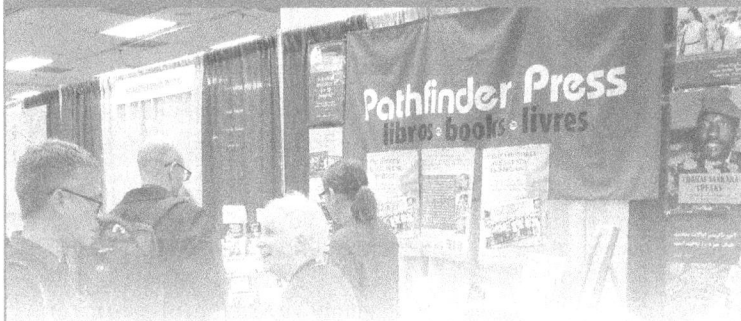

UNITED STATES
(and Caribbean, Latin America, and East Asia)

Pathfinder Books, 306 W. 37th St., 13th Floor
New York, NY 10018

CANADA

Pathfinder Books, 7107 St. Denis, Suite 204
Montreal, QC H2S 2S5

UNITED KINGDOM
(and Europe, Africa, Middle East, and South Asia)

Pathfinder Books, 5 Norman Rd.
Seven Sisters, London N15 4ND

AUSTRALIA
(and New Zealand, Southeast Asia, and the Pacific)

Pathfinder Books, Suite 2, First floor, 275 George St.
Liverpool, Sydney, NSW 2170
Postal address: P.O. Box 73, Campsie, NSW 2194

BUILD YOUR LIBRARY!
JOIN THE PATHFINDER READERS CLUB

$10 / YEAR
25% DISCOUNT ON ALL PATHFINDER TITLES
30% OFF BOOKS OF THE MONTH
Valid at pathfinderpress.com and local Pathfinder book centers

Go to: pathfinderpress.com/
products/pathfinder-readers-club

Pathfinder
pathfinderpress.com